I0892959

THE VERY MAN

Also by Charles Boyle from Carcanet

Sleeping Rough

Charles Boyle

The Very Man

CARCANET

First published in 1993 by
Carcanet Press Limited
208-212 Corn Exchange Buildings
Manchester M4 3BQ

A CIP catalogue record for this book
is available from the British Library.
ISBN 0 85635 955 6

The publisher acknowledges financial assistance
from the Arts Council of Great Britain.

Set in 10pt Palatino by Bryan Williamson, Frome
Printed and bound in England by SRP Ltd, Exeter

Arts Council Funded

A foolish man rides here
with my saddle
and on my camel.

'In the Heart of the Desert' by Al-Tirimmah (?660-?725),
translated by Omar Pound

Acknowledgements

Poems in this collection were first printed in: *London Magazine, London Review of Books, New Statesman, Poetry London Newsletter, PN Review, Times Literary Supplement*. 'Cartography' was a prize-winner in the 1991 Arvon competition.

'Kronsverskaya Prospekt' (Maxim Gorky's address in 1919) borrows details from Tania Alexander, *An Estonian Childhood* (1987). 'Frog Prince' is indebted to the translation by David Ellis of Stendhal's *Memoirs of an Egotist*.

Contents

Timur the Lame

A man with a limp came towards me,
begging money for liquor – spoke of cairns
built of skulls, of the wind off the steppes
on the night before battle
and the evils of cholesterol.

Some of this, I thought, he must be making up.
Besides, what was I doing here,
talking with a dead Mongol warrior,
in the middle of the life that was mine?

At the end of the street, some camels
grazing, the air mottled with flies
above ribbons of goat flesh...
Even the tourists looked sick.
Even the women, that day, were not untouched.

He said: You think a life
has a beginning, middle and end?
Then he emptied his pockets
and showed me the eyes of Hafiz.

Arlington Mansions

Towards midnight on my thirtieth birthday
I was teasing a 5-amp fuse wire
between a pair of recalcitrant screws,
remembering in the dark
April 12, 1961: Yuri Gagarin, first man alive
to see the whole blue ball in space,
and myself aged ten in the back of a car
being driven east.

A dog came scratching for food.
A bowl of cold chicken curry later,
I half-led, half-pushed it back home
to the gaga lady upstairs –
the Flower Girl, the Millionairess,
former star of the silent screen –
who lived on chocolate and cigarettes.

Sshhh, she whispered, one finger on her lips,
the same sound of the sea
I could hear beyond Flamborough Head.

Man in Space

No, I said, the title isn't sexist,
I was thinking about the Russian cosmonauts
who were stuck in orbit, and how the ground-crew hooked up a
 British princess
and an interpreter
and got them to make polite conversation.

Then there was Daniel, who wanted a child
but whose girlfriend didn't.
After five years of precautions
he began sleeping with another woman.

The night he told me she was pregnant
and that he didn't love her, he told me also
his recurring dream: he's tobogganing
down this hill he remembers, it was called the Death Trap –
near the bottom you had to make a sharp turn
and steer through a gate, if you failed
you smashed into a fence.

Now he's gathering speed, going faster and faster...
And suddenly there's nothing there, just snow
upon snow upon snow.

I poured us another glass. And the child too, I told him,
like an illegal immigrant, stowed away
in darkness, among the crates of Old World cheeses
and bits of machinery, en route to the promised land.
You have to make that arrival good.

He said it's not like that, it's all refrigerated
containers. We argued
about the transport of whisky, and about the girls of America.

A Piece of His Mind

What does he think about, I can see them wondering,
the women who look at Edwin
after he's told them his favourite statistic –
that the average man thinks about sex
for one in every fifteen minutes –
for the other fourteen?
A little faith, a little charity and hope?

(Think of three bald men, an aunt once told me:
a cure for hiccups. It didn't work,
any more than drinking from a cup's wrong side
or holding my breath till it hurt.)

He had noticed, he once told me, seeing celebrities
ducking into or out of taxis, they're always smaller
than he'd expected. He had fallen in love
so often...

We were walking
in winter in the City, past the yellow-lit
tinny interiors
behind the black nineteenth-century façades.
Even these, he said, were significant details.

Even Ledyard, he said, the explorer John Ledyard,
who determined
to take America by surprise from the west,
even Ledyard reached Omsk, Tomsk and Kachuga
and floated downriver to Irkutsk
before he got caught and deported
by Catherine the Great.

Frog Prince

Am I good or bad, clever or stupid?
Stendhal asks himself
in the summer of 1832.

A life of falling in love and off horses...
Carriage wheels on cobbles, a rattle
of distant muskets: it's half past one

in the morning and already too hot to think
or sleep, yet eleven hundred pretty women a year –
he has seen the official statistics –

leaving the ballrooms of Paris at dawn
are catching colds from which they die.
Meanwhile the Duke of Frioul

at the age of thirty-eight – 'the age when,'
as Stendhal himself remarks, 'if one is disillusioned,
boredom begins to appear on the horizon' –

is strolling about, alone and slightly drunk,
in the gloom of the Palais Royal gardens,
where a boy is catching frogs

for the knife of Dr Edwards, an Englishman,
who seeks a cure for the women's complaint
and to discover how we breathe.

The Harrow Road

Seeing snow for the very first time,
she ran out into the street
in her Wimpy costume
and had her wages docked.

Slower and lighter than rain, different
from how she'd imagined it...

The black, humped shape
her room-mate made with a boyfriend
made her think of Oscar Wilde,
his *Collected Works* on her father's shelf
brought back from this city
before she was conceived.

Kronsverskaya Prospekt

One week there is nothing but apples,
the next week herring
and the next cabbages, most of them already rotten.

Anna brings home the cabbages
and makes a stew for ten or a dozen people.
Then they talk into the night
about the masterpieces of world literature
they are even now translating,
the plays they will put on
and how the shapes of even spoons and forks
will be changed by the new perspective.

Moura and Mariussa are standing by the window.
What Moura's caught sight of
is a house in the country with running water
where people she doesn't know
are eating meat and fresh bread – then a cloud
scuds across the moon.

Mariussa who is the youngest of all
and will be the last to die, if allowed to live out
the span of his natural life, Mariussa too
is still hungry, he is tracing his own disappearance –
eyes, hair, nose, lips –
with his finger on the wet pane.

The Chess Player

I'm thinking of a famous grandmaster
on the sixteenth floor of a hotel in Bucharest,
kept awake by the gypsy music
of a wedding party downstairs.

I'm seeing him watch from his window
some cleaning women emerge
in the sodium-lit small hours
from the national exhibition centre,
and the rails from the station stretching
towards the vanishing point of asylum.

When at last he falls asleep
to the strains of the last violin,
he dreams fitfully
of a lady with a parasol
stepping out on the first marble square
of a black and white chequered piazza.

His task is to guide her across
to the shade of the colonnade
before history takes over,
before the city lies in ruins.

The light is hot and even
and, like the Pyramids when they were built,
the stones are so perfectly cut
a knife blade couldn't slip between them.

(1988)

The Letter Writer

When they entered the private apartments
they found wall-to-wall wardrobes of Paris clothes
and a room made into a cinema
for watching favourite American films.

Caesar also, with Calpurnia,
no doubt whiled winter evenings away
with wine, musicians and foreign dancers
as I too enjoy American films... Soldiers
lined up in a square, a crowd of civilians –
then someone gives the order, and they fire.

Later, scenes of public rejoicing
as the border is opened...
Meanwhile, a man we have learnt to care about
is searching among the fallen
for a young girl – there is always a sub-plot
with a young and beautiful girl.

She lives alone in a block of flats.
Her brother has been killed.
It is evening and the electricity has been cut off
and she is writing fast: *I want to tell you*
about that church behind the stadium,
when they unlocked the door...

Here I see her pause and look up,
glancing over her shoulder
as if there were someone else in the room.
But there is no one, it is only a noise in the street.

Fault Line

There was so much right on both sides,
Ken said, we could each found a church,
and the people who stuck by whichever holy writ
would be people he wouldn't mind meeting.

At the time, I was kneeling on the floor
with a self-assembly bookshelves kit,
wondering why they'd given me only nine nuts
for ten bolts, and just when he'd said that,

about the two churches, I realized
that the alarm bell on the used-car garage
which had been ringing since Friday night
had stopped. For the first time for years

I felt a shiver run through me
and into the ground. Then Ken was saying,
in his seen-it-all, done-it-all voice,
Have you ever watched a priest, a priest

in full regalia, in tears? Weeping's
the word, not crying, and the snotty grey handkerchief
he keeps up the sleeve of his vestment
can't stem the waters of Babylon.

I Didn't Mean to Kill My Husband

she said, and I believed her, as we came out of Finnegan's
at nine o'clock on a rainy evening
and headed for somewhere to eat. Water was running
down the roofs and gutters
like the Nile in flood, and when she closed her blue, blue eyes
when we kissed,
I knew she was the kind of person
who just lets what will happen happen, as I was too.

Cartography

Miles back, we had taken a wrong turning.
Fields, fields without sheep or cattle, and the oncoming traffic
repeated themselves in a continuous loop
and I thought perhaps you were sulking but no,
you said, just thinking, wondering in fact
where that passage in Lawrence was
about nothing being left in the world
except himself and a rabbit – was it in *Apocalypse*
or in the Penguin selection from *Phoenix*?

Rain was spotting the windscreen, not enough for the wipers,
and your small rounded toes
where you'd kicked off your shoes
under what I still called the glove compartment
were clenching then more slowly unclenching...
We were headed towards some infamous inn
in the middle of nowhere – until a warning sign,
ESTATE FARM SHOP 200 YARDS, and I slowed
and then parked on the gravel outside.

Tea-towels and pottery mugs and recipe books
in what had once been a barn, now lit
with fluorescent bulbs. In-laws, you said,
or wicked stepmothers, is who this stuff is for.
A freezer held packs of fish and game
'flown in yesterday from Scotland,' according to the girl
when she'd turned down her Walkman. And opening
the lid, I felt the chill of Mercator: the globe
sliced open and ruled, splayed on a cut-and-dried page.

Snow in September

After dinner, her husband excused himself:
he had some cheques to sign.
He had travelled widely,
and in the lounge where we sat for coffee

there was a prayer mat on the wall,
a drum, spears and a wood figurine,
its arms clasped above its head
and something white like seashells for eyes.

All that was before they'd met, she said,
tucking her legs beside her, picking fluff
from her dress. When he was married
to someone else. I began to talk

about life as a teacher abroad, about role-play
situations and a passage from Darwin
which even after I'd explained the vocab
might as well have been in Greek.

I drew a line round the classroom walls
as long as the life of this planet;
at the end of this line I marked off an inch,
the span of human existence.

This confirmed their belief I was mad.
What they wanted was irregular verbs
and jobs with American companies.
But they smiled, it amused them, and her.

And the snow, snow in September?

Come and see for yourself, she said,
looking out from the patio door
across their garden and the garden opposite,
and tell me about the one you were in love with.

Lion Cub

Lost in the garden suburbs, where the sprinklers
swung idly on lawns and the bored, incurious sentries
with loaded carbines

regarded us passing: two men and one girl
out on the town... Raising the spirit
of competition.

There were all-night bars
where the players and dancers from the nightclubs around
came to drink between sessions

with the second sons of the newly rich;
car chases along the Corniche,
swimming nude in the Sporting Club pool;

a diminishing row of clay cups
on the table before me, in the hashish parlour
I never found again in daylight.

The bouncers
who had us leave the nightclub
where we emptied the floor by dancing *à trois* –

and the casino at the Sheraton,
and the private apartment in Zamalek
where the lion cub went missing –

worked as a team, polite but strict
as the parents of an only child
who is going to get somewhere in life.

Canaries

I was in love that summer – it is worth something
to be young and in love
in a foreign city.

Everything was rounded and just touching
like the curves in the wrought-iron grille
above my apartment door.
I thought: there may be something more to life
than this, but not much more.

Walking home in the late afternoon
down a street of workshops, mechanics' dens, stray dogs
and sometimes sheep, as I neared the shop
that sold caged birds
I'd shut my eyes – to hear
as if underground the canaries singing.

First Draft

Mitzi told all: what they liked
best, how quick they'd be about it,
the blotches on their skin. He
could imagine this.

What he couldn't understand
was the point of the joke the proprietor told
every time he came in,
about an Englishman and a biscuit.

Then up to his room with its dusty
pink lampshade – was this what they meant
by rose-tinted spectacles? –
and the sheets unchanged for three weeks.

*

Next, himself and B. Traven
whooping it up in the backroom.
Next, a priest with a Latin swan song
curdling the blood-bath dénouement.

He packed hurriedly, in darkness,
then ran through the backstreets
to the waiting ship... Later,
in the light summer nights of the north,

he'd sit out on a spartan verandah,
a dog curled at his feet
and Mitzi making sense
of his cross-hatched long-hand scrawl.

Cannibals

Tomorrow, the boy says, the boy who's been to school
in Eskisehir... It could be next week.
And she knows what tonight will bring:
a stew with bits of gristle, a mattress above the garage
where their car is being repaired
with parts from another.

There was once, her husband tells her, an archaeologist
at a dig not far from here.
Children started throwing stones –
he picked one up and threw it back.
Then a man appeared and shot him dead
with a gun you could have auctioned at Sotheby's.

How do you know? she says.
Meaning, that the gun was so valuable?
Meaning, why should I believe you
when you say it'll all be all right,
when you say today is Tuesday
and that you love me?

Then the racket starts up again, metal
dinning on metal, the flare of a welder's torch,
and she turns to stare at the boy –
clothes several sizes too big,
something knowing but weak in the eyes –
the boy who can read and write.

Expat

An address I can't pronounce, a divan,
a teach-yourself Arabic, a draft
of his time-and-motion report and a girl named Susan
arrived from the airport with whisky and cornflakes.

One night, after too much drinking,
she gets up at dawn for a pee
and sees or dreams through the bathroom window
a sheep being killed by two men.

It's some festival, she thinks.

It's some festival, he tells her
over the cornflakes. They've been invited
by a neighbour, a man high up in the national bank,
to break the fast with his family.

Something yellow goes by in the street...
There are people they both know still mowing the lawn
and walking the dog; wives, mortgages
in the middle distance, an enormous sum.

Stone, Paper, Scissors

Adze, sickle, potsherd, flint: her lips
shaping the words into sounds
he'd never heard, a song of independence.

A postcard from Muscat, Oman:
she'd met someone who worked on the rigs,
who didn't correct her grammar.

Then nothing for years, just the heat
and the insects' singing, until he heard
she was in New York, working for the U.N.

This happened in the place where he'd
brought her, off the dirt road to the falls,
over neat whisky and while cutting out

the crossword – the white squares filled in,
the answers slowly pieced together
around the black ones – to send back home.

Both Sides of the River

Watching dustclouds through a rainblurred window
in the cheaper part of town,
he cut out a Masai warrior
from a book on African history.

His children were initiated
at the correct age
into alcohol, cars and sex.
His wife assumed he'd gone hunting
but this time, she decided, she would sit it out:
no asking who was that on the phone,
no reading of letters in pockets.

Moving from kraal to kraal,
enjoying his several women,
he recited the names of his cattle
and of trees, rivers and plants...
Often he'd get stuck at *alimony*
and have to start all over again.

The simple life is neither here nor there –
a spare room, or just the corner of a room,
the horizon stretched to its limits.

from *A Cast of Thousands*

A New Man

Cut here: ——— Fold here: – – – –
Stand upright in front of window.
See the light shine through his ears.

Secretary

'Have you ever, really, known what it means, to be
in love?' Her fingers stall, perhaps
a quarter of an inch above the keyboard.

An Alpine Scene

'Doctor, I have this friend...'
Sunshine and melting snow: a picture of innocence
on last month's page of the drug-company calendar.

Ex-Secretary

She'd be singing the songs
from forties musicals,
and when she didn't know the words she'd hum.

Blossom

I'm in Waterstones, where they know about these things,
I'm trying to buy a book with the word *Tree*
in its title, I forget the author, it's something
I've been told I must read by someone I trust,
over a week ago now, and the girl at the desk,
the cashier, pretty, brunette, is on the phone
to a friend, who is causing some problem about tonight's
arrangements, nine o'clock in the Yorkshire Grey,
and while nestling the phone to her cheek, between her ear
and left shoulder, a trick I could never manage,
is taking money from the person, woman, in front of me,
giving one pound and five pee change, then dropping the book,
six hundred pages at least, with a palm tree, black
palm tree, not the same tree at all, and embossed
gold letters on its cover, into a purple plastic bag,
adding bookmark, receipt, a smile, a frank
and beautiful smile, still insisting that Stephen and Julie
are leaving tomorrow, it could be their last chance ever.

From a 94 Bus

The children of the rich are girls aged four or five
riding in the backs of cars with fast acceleration
should the need arise which it rarely does.
Tied loosely round their necks are straw or felt hats with ribbons.

Their teeth and skin and hair are without blemish.
Their tantrums are the stuff of legend, ditto their *sang froid*.
Without ever having spoken to them or come within earshot
battalions have died with these girls' names on their lips.

Already they know everything there is to be known about money
  and sex
and they know that they know it. In the crooks of their little fingers
is written the history of their class and whether their brothers
prosper or go to the dogs makes no difference at all.

Wherever they will arrive they are expected.

An Asian Supermarket

There she goes on her travels again,
very tall with her ash-blonde hair
among the smiling Kashmiri boatmen.
Fair enough, he thinks, she needs a change of air.

Now she's leading a campaign for someone's rights.
Becoming a Buddhist.
Exploiting the gap in the market: selling weeds,
for example, which can be just as beautiful
as certain flowers she could name.

Hold on, he says, haven't we been here before?
– One, maybe two cigarettes downstairs, alone,
then she comes back to bed

where she tries but knows she will fail to fall asleep
until she remembers what it was
she forgot to buy: a something that glints,
non-biodegradable, down the aisle
snagged with lianas, past the crumbling
spirit-guardians at the check-out desks.

Weekend: A Scenario

Friday to Sunday, and so much so she feared forever,
from arriving tired to the booked pink room
with a view of the car park, the rain, the intervals
between the rain, the bed, the table, the dog, slobbering,
in the bar, until the minutes, after they'd packed,
when she opened and closed every drawer, then went down
on all fours to check under the bed for something
she might have missed, while he stood in the doorway,
impatient, bored, with the car keys in his hand.

The Office Suite

1 *Bifocals*

He asked if I'd had a good journey
and how I saw myself in ten years' time.

Balding, bifocals, his name
and title stencilled on the door –
I was supposed to look him straight back
and say: 'Sitting where you are now.'

What were the long-term prospects
for literature in the video age?
And how, we wondered,
had our single mutual acquaintance
made such a mess of his brilliant future?
. . . Staring the while
at the brick wall opposite
where the rain gave itself away
in splinters of light.

I couldn't do it . . . I recalled
the man on the Underground
of about my own age,
methodically tearing an advert for mouthwash
into smaller and smaller pieces.

Depilatory cream and pregnancy testing
would be the next to go.
I'd committed their texts to heart
rather than meet his eyes.

He kept calling the new librarian
by the name of the one
before the one she'd replaced...

And sometimes in mid-afternoon, returning
from the Taj Mahal or the Café Venezia,
he stepped out of the lift
on the wrong floor.

Someone would have to lead him back
to his own desk, where he'd regret
not having crossed Iran
when the borders were open.

*

Three hours into the Christmas party
he was found in reception, talking
with the night security guard
about the politics of underdevelopment.

Come on up, someone said, the fun's just beginning.
No, he replied, all that's for you youngsters –
synchronizing his exit
through the revolving doors

with the entry of a Japanese tourist
who won first prize in the raffle:
a hostess trolley.

3 Writ in Water

Across from our office was another
like ours, but whose whole façade
was made of glass. No pane was
exactly true, and on clear mornings our late
arrivals, hangovers, feet
on desks and industrious moments
were reflected there as if in water.

Later, when they switched on their lights,
the glass gave way
like the front of an old dolls' house.
There were the serious men in suits
and the secretaries at their keyboards,
and the man who clears memos from out-trays
to redistribute in in-trays.

A vent at the top uttered steam and,
one day in early spring, a brimming froth of suds
which the lightest breeze creamed off.

4 *Chronicle*

In the Year of the Ape, 1404,
for a single night
all bans were cancelled, everything was licensed.
All the dancing girls of Asia.

I remember the face of the new office temp
as she looked towards me,
then back to her VDU – a face so blank, so wrapped
in the ghost-noise of her Walkman,

I might equally have been her boyfriend
or Tamburlaine the Great
before he died of exhaustion
en route to China.

5 *The Whites of Their Eyes*

Count Corner at Borodino, at 4 p.m.
on 7 September 1812:
'Is this damn battle never going to finish?'
40,000 Russians and 30,000 Frenchmen
lay dead or dying around him...

So it is these weekday afternoons –
feeling drowsy and at the same time restless,
wanting this thing to be over –
when Johnson comes in and gives me a look.

Up on the roof for a smoke, here's London
on parade: a race of small-boned people
threading through the eyes of streets,
stitching their lives into place.

Blink, and it's Moscow in flames –
and there's Johnson and me
up to our knees in snow
on the winter retreat.

6 The Wine-Dark Excursion

Discos, air-conditioned tavernas, a patch of scrub land
with goats, between half-built motels...
But the wine was good wine, and the brandy,
and somewhere they stopped at a garage
with a single petrol pump
and a mechanic who washed their windscreen –

A small town in the foothills
where the men marry the girls next door
and on the whole stay faithful,
bringing up their families
to a life that is not that different
from how it was, when they were children.

A bunch of wankers, commented Marketing,
whose English was near-perfect,
as he opened another bottle. One of the Sales girls
had fallen asleep, her friend
had begun to cry. So Accounts took the wheel
and steered them back home, or a place not too unlike,

where tomorrow they would sit in rows
in a curtained room
while a projector beamed record profits
and the Chairman thanked them all for a job well done.

See How They Run

Reverse, forward and stall. Reverse and stall.
I must have looked like the late beginner
at the dancing class in Pudsey
who got stuck without a partner.

On the High Street at last,
having mastered the six-point turn,
we were doing about 40
when my instructor slapped his left knee, the sign
for an emergency stop.

Or was it the three giggling bridesmaids
decked out in blue satin,
tripping down the steps from a boarded-up house?

Crawley Welcomes Careful Drivers

I'd have lived opposite the Esso garage, where they put
the tiger in your tank. I'd have had three aunts –
Alice, Joan and the other one, who married beneath her –
a Hornby train set, a yoyo, a tree house, a military badge.

An only child, I'd have been allowed to stay up to watch the news.
Sometimes I would have wondered if my parents were really
my parents, and would have imagined sailing to Rio
to find my true father and meeting him in the stock exchange,

easily the tallest man there. Until then, I'd have fished
for sticklebacks with Jeremy, my friend. *His* father, something
in insurance, would have smoked a pipe with a curvy stem.
And one night, having talked about it for weeks, Jeremy

would have gone and done it: next morning, the assistant pro
would have found the bank manager's Jaguar crashed into a tree
off the eighteenth fairway and, lying on the back seat, asleep,
apparently unharmed, the bank manager's lovely naked daughter.

Around that time, I'd have opted for geography and economics.
I'd have worried about God and checked every nook and cranny for signs
of hereditary disease. Jeremy would have gone up to Oxford.
I'd have learnt how to foxtrot with his younger sister.

The End of the World

was scheduled for noon on the fifth of February.
This was Peter Schroeder's thirteenth birthday.
His parents arrived mid-morning
with parcels and a cake, then drove off in their Jag
past the gate-house lodge
where the Latin master and the assistant matron
were living in sin.

The last lesson before lunch
began at a quarter to twelve. Forty minutes later
the prefect on duty rang the bell.

The cake, I remember, was yellow,
pink and green sponge, and the candles were snuffed
with a single puff. Things were beginning
to add up. Next September, Peter and I
would be going to different schools.
Later, I'd be a pilot in the RAF
and Peter would take over his father's soft-drinks company.

That summer we drank the new Schroeder Cola.
The label on each bottle showed a girl
drinking from a bottle, on which there was a girl, etc.

A Swish of Organza

After the war, what was to be done
was to build the world anew
for the children that kept getting born.

Labour, then the fruits of labour...
Then the children shut their bedroom doors
and began to 'experiment'.

Each summer, my uncle and aunt took to water,
a cruise in the Med
where they dressed for dinner
and stopped off at the ancient ports,
returning with souvenirs.

There was dancing, and there were tables for bridge.
One night, a stranger asked if they'd mind
if he drew up a chair and watched.
When my aunt retired to bed,
he was asked to make a fourth.

I imagine my uncle's serious look
across the green baize, waiting for his partner's bid
as the ship holds steady on course.
An Englishman's code: things hinted
and understood, cards played close to the chest.

The stranger was Mantovani.
Now they are alone in the bar, and Mantovani explains
how he sold his first million,
how he invented the cascading strings.
Then back to the hotel days –
success isn't cheaply bought, he says,
though luck plays a part, and chancing the odds,
it comes down in the end to hard work.

A night to remember. I think of my uncle
taking a last turn on deck, the bright
constellations above, the white of the sea spilling by.
And my aunt asleep below,
and the engines' muffled beat.

Beauty Spot

You were dancing with a wasp...
Yet again, the small mole
to the right of and just below your lips
which they said would make people love you
hadn't worked.

Something else besides
tucked into the landscape, doomed
and heroic
as the Charge of the Light Brigade.

The Futures Market

What's *higado*? Liver, or courage.
And *ternera a la flamenca*?
Service is slow, there's football

on the TV, I'm trying to explain
to this girl with green eyes
why I'm not from Ireland, though I have an Irish name.

Say a man has to leave his village in a hurry,
he takes a horse and then a boat
and that's as far as his money takes him.

So he hires himself out to a local farmer,
a widower with a pretty daughter, and because he's good
with animals, he's used to their smells

and warmth, he's asked to stay on
for the winter... But then the fish
turns out to be veal, which she doesn't eat

on principle, the away team equalize
in a goalmouth scramble
in the final minute, and we go into extra time.

The Very Man

I'd stopped for a bite in Alfredo's
when I saw myself walking by
in the coat I wore all last winter –
not shabby, not yet quite over the hill,
but hardly the man of the moment
I'd taken myself to be.

The least I could do was to call out my name
and ask if I'd heard any news
from a girl we both used to know.
Oh her, came the answer, she's fine –
but something I sensed in the tone of my voice
made the words not ring wholly true.

That night I reappeared, calling at the house
to take you out. I wanted to warn you,
to say this man's another man than he seems,
but you were too eager
or I was too slow
and before I could speak you had gone.

A Time of One's Life

Breakfast silver service in the one-time ballroom,
waited on by a young Greek boy and his likely grandfather.
Its decor is tangerine-pink, the steady reflected light

of forest fires inland... Afternoons peter out
along unmade roads leading nowhere gently uphill –
you might think poor, from the drowned donkey

damming the canal, from the small blackened circles on the verges
where fires have been lit for a purpose,
but you'd be wrong: bougainvillaea billows

over walls three feet thick, padlocked gates, and the maddened dogs
behind them wear studded collars.
(More here than anywhere, a feeling of being watched,

of it simply not being done
to take photographs or ask where the money comes from.)
I keep thinking of leaving and inventing excuses,

like falling in love with the six-times life-size hand-painted girl
in the ad for brandy on the airport road, in a dress
that puts (as if it cared) the flat black sea to shame.

Ten Minutes from the City

We start at the top: the master bedroom
with en suite bathroom. And with, by the bed,
a gleaming chrome exercise machine
on which a man is cycling
down a sandy path
towards a hut made of reeds and mud...

In the smallest bedroom, a child is asleep.
Keeping the light switched off
in case it might wake him, we stare out above the cot
into trees and homecoming traffic.

In the kitchen, Elke, the Dutch au pair, is reading
the evening paper and chain-smoking Gauloises.
She is waiting for the telephone to ring.
There's a smell of burning, and this woman
who is showing me her life
hurries to the cooker, then she takes a cloth
to wipe up the mess
in which the twins, her older children, have sat.

They need more space, she says.
They are moving to the country.
They are open to offers – I must talk
with her husband, who should be home any minute.

I keep thinking about that hut, the sound
that comes from inside, and the man not getting any nearer
however hard he pedals... He's there
again, sitting across the table, where a dinner party
is in full swing – late forties,
tired, pouring a glass of red wine.

He is explaining the domino theory.
He clears a space among the dishes
and stands three books upright,
about three inches apart.
Then he pushes the nearest book
with his finger, and they all fall down.

So clearly do I imagine this
I can read the spines of the books... His children,
now in their teens, have seen it all before.

Small Print

There's not a house in England, said my grandfather,
surveyor and auctioneer, without something in it
of value... What brought him to mind was the patter
of the blue-eyed agent, young enough to be my own son,
making light of the broken windows, leaking roof
and patches of damp. And the attic I escaped to,
a room like the deck of a ship, the *Marie Celeste*,
with a mug of warm tea and a paper – where I read
of another royal birth, suspected foul play and a granny
in Tetford, Lincs., who had handed in an unexploded
grenade which had stood on the mantelpiece since 1918.

Breeze Block

She kisses him and takes the keys.
He sits on the steps and lights
a cigarette while she
sees what's inside.

A pile of dead leaves.
A room with a view of the same room again.
A box of teeth, a conversation about God.
A goat strung up from a tripod of sticks
being skinned by another goat.

'... it's not as if
it's for the rest of our lives –'

(She hadn't heard him come in.)

He goes out to the balcony
and tries to light another cigarette,
but the wind keeps blowing out his matches.

Squatting there on his haunches.

Lost, Stolen or Strayed
she remembers, a book she'd once read
about a dog.

The Wren

All that day, beginning hot, they'd set out
to find Cocteau's grave,
he couldn't help seeing
the tiny bruise on her throat
where her necklace, she said, had got caught.

The weather broke, the grave
turned out to be Braque's,
her shoes were a size too small...

Home and dry, she peeled off her socks
and showed him the rubbed-red patch,
about the size of a farthing,
where a blister had formed, and expired.

The Anniversary

While she is putting in her contact lenses
he remembers the Liberator bomber –
the tiny ball-turret gunners
sealed in their perspex domes; the grey plastic pieces
he'd snapped off the stem, then glued
and assembled and painted... smoothing down the transfer
of Marion or Carole
on the fuselage, just below the cockpit.

What's the fate of perfect scale models
except to get mislaid?
They had taken the honeymoon suite
in an effort to cheer themselves up.

Bed, brocade, those huntsmen leaping hedges.
Sometimes, he thinks – watching, in sunshine after rain,
beyond the lawn laid out for croquet
and a field with sheep,
another field being churned into mud
by a cyclocross – there is nothing to add
to what is already here.

He opens the window a fraction,
to hear the bikes crash gears and thunder.

Until the woman shivers, and the day-glo anoraks
that pepper the verges
dissolve into a rainbow, an arrow
bent through the air
from Scythia, he recalls, or Parthia,
a desert country, an arrow zeroed in
on a heart carved in the bark of a tree
where *x* LOVES *y*
still begs the other half of the equation.

An Early Night

All the flights tonight are fully booked
by women in creaseproof dresses
nursing neat brandies
in their tried and trusted laps.

A shadow trembling on the asphalt,
the night-nurse come with her teaspoon of linctus –
the Lady with the Lamp, I call her,
but her expression doesn't change.

Time to loosen my Indian belt, time to unpack
the expensive shirt – to twist
the stiff cardboard
from under the collar, to unpick the pins.

Early Photographs

In the nineteenth, surely the saddest century yet,
I was a boy standing alone and very still
in the corridor of a gothic institution
of the type built to house poor orphans or the mad.

I was Darwin in the Galapagos
riding a tortoise, on the brink of my big idea.
I was the fair-skinned man in Arabia Deserta
about whom Doughty, travelling later, heard rumours.

I was a pig-tailed Chinese pirate
slamming down the railroad
across the US prairies.
I was beside myself with hope, anger, fear and exhaustion.

Suddenly, and at exactly the same time,
a bird in the grounds
makes its fatuous trill, and the boy
waggles his head very fast from side to side.

Eadweard Muybridge

'My name is Muybridge,' said the night-time visitor,
'and I have a message for you from my wife.'
Then he fired a single shot

from a Smith & Wesson No. 2…
The women sitting, the men discussing
in low voices, the future rushing in

from left to right margin, then back to the left –
after Major Harry Larkyns had staggered back,
trailed blood through the house and out the back door,

Muybridge apologised to the ladies.
He lent his carriage to fetch a doctor
and sat down in the parlour with a newspaper.

I'd kill a man like that myself if I had to.
Sleep some hours in the afternoon, take a shower
and a gun and do it. And afterwards

– acquitted, on the grounds of Larkyns
having got his deserts – continue my experiment
involving horses, birds, male and female nudes, children

from the Blockley Hospital for the Poor,
trip wires and batteries of cameras
with shutter speeds of 1/1000th of a second.

Scan

The colours of the nurses' uniforms were: blue
blue and white, almond-blossom pink
with a sort of (optional) white cap with frills
Florence Nightingale might have worn
amid the mire and gore of Scutari.

They walked with a purpose,
calling out names from clipboard lists.

Were we the chosen? That day
of February's cold snap, all else
blanked out by snow, we watched on the screen
mini-astronauts
turning somersaults inside you,
testing the laws
of gravity and the sublime.

*

Aged five, I rode piggy-back
on my father's shoulders
into the foundry, and screamed
to be taken out.

Shadrach, Meshach and Abednego
in my scripture notebook...

After he died, my mother switched off the engine
at the top of Harewood Hill.
We freewheeled down
in a silence that made me invisible.

*

I brooded in cafés, diminished
by a three-year ban
on the plural of 'child'.

We argued fiercely – why?
To come nearer my own father? To make up
for bad verse? *Why not*?

Once, exhausted, silenced, I looked aside
at the ten o'clock news –
a landscape under several feet of water,
telegraph poles at odd angles,
families on the roofs of their separate homes
waiting to be rescued.

*

An idea for a story, a memory of a story:
a man arrives in a town
with an important message
on which everything else depends.
He takes a room above a café
like the room in Arles, and after a few days –
hot, dry days and nights that are cold –
still no one has approached him.
Just the man and his bird, pecking
on the floor of its cage.

That's the gist. The rest is in the telling:
the dirt between his toes, how he falls down
one day in the street, the light
low-slanting
across a northern estuary
I once crossed by ferry, for just twenty minutes or so
while I stood at the rail and watched
small islands slipping by, some rocks and sheep,
the kind of islands rich men buy
for a hobby, or to start a new life.

*

Waters broke, and we drove
not speaking, not daring to interrupt
the windscreen wipers' heartbeat rhythm.

Too red and wet to be true
they arrived
in a four-square sixth-floor room –
rain applauded
on all the roofs of west London.

*

On the one hand and on the other.
Brown eyes and blue, round and pointed ears.

Let down from my arms, they hurry on all fours
to the edge of the lake, and sit there
licking stones
or throwing them a little way
into the water – the fish darting
almost within my grasp...

When I think of my father
in the years before I was born
he's both hardly there
and so close we overlap – on holiday
with friends, somewhere foreign with mountains,
being called inside
from a wooden balcony.

Once I wanted to be an architect.
(I wish now I'd become a doctor.)

Later I wrote stories
about characters named Mark or Paul
who went on journeys
and either died in tragic circumstance
or returned home.

I think I knew then I would always write
but not so I'd earn my living from it.

*

For a day when I'm eighty
and they are my own age now
I'm photographing my children
on the grass in the park.

The hottest May
since records began. Planes
like enormous fish
just over the treetops
towards Heathrow. And everywhere children –
with their parents whose lives have utterly changed
or with foreign girls
they'll hardly remember.

Mine keep their best, their world-
enveloping smiles
for the moment just after I've pressed the shutter.

– How does the plane
stay up in the sky? Why doesn't it fall
into the trees? I've still
only the foggiest notion.

Last Seen

Early forties, medium build, jeans, dark jacket
and bearing in mind the words of late Stendhal
– 'In anything involving women, I am fortunate enough
to be as easily deceived
as I was at twenty-five' – I tighten the straps
of my sagging rucksack and round the corner

into kingdom come. Where a teasing wind
flaps shirts on a line
this way then that. Where a taxi slows to a crawl,
checking house numbers, and a man returns home
to find – no press of suitors, faithful wife or dog –
letters from his children postmarked Troy.